Images

of

Seattle

This book features the photography of
James Blank
Robert Shangle
Charlie Borland

Revised Edition
First Printing October, 1991
Published By LTA Publishing Company
Division of Renaissance Publishing Company, Inc.
318 East 7th Street, Auburn,IN 46706

Concept and Design: Robert D. Shangle

Library of Congress Cataloging-in-Publication Data
Images of Seattle / concept and design, Robert D. Shangle.
p.   cm.   ISBN 1-55988-350-2: (soft bound):$6.95
1. Seattle (Wash.) —Description.— Views. I. Shangle, Robert D. da.
F899.S443I43   1991   917.97'772 —dc20   91-35042 CIP

Introduction

"What a beautiful area! " "I want to remember this forever!" "It's absolutely awesome!" "The Creator simply out-did Himself!"

All of these statements are descriptive of the thoughts expressed when viewing this great city of Seattle that we live in, work in, and play in. And why not. This is a Grand Place.

Images linger in our mind's eye, bringing back those memories of excitement, happiness, family, loved ones, places we've visited, or always dreamed of visiting. One can remember, either because "I've been there," or visited vicariously. We want to hold onto those experiences of "places I've been, things I've done, places I want to see."

The images in this book have been gathered together to assist with those memories and you can give it life. Combining these pictures with your memories make them fill with energy, telling your story that is full of excitement and thrills.

A tribute to Seattle!

The Space Needle

Pacific Science Center at Seattle Center

Seattle Skyline

Seattle Skyline

Salmon Bay Harbor

Japanese Gardens in University of Washington Arboretum

Lake Union and the Seattle Skyline

Seattle Skyline from Waterfront Park

The "Pike Place Hillclimb"

The Space Needle at Seattle Center

Freeway Park

Green Lake

Pick Place Public Market

The Kingdome

Hiram Chittenden Locks on Lake Washington Ship Canal

Seattle Skyline

Along the Waterfront

On top of the Space Needle

Shilshole Bay

Lake Union from the top of the Space Needle

Elliott Bay and Mount Rainier

"Trolley" Service Along the Waterfront

Waterfall Earden

Mount Rainier

Along the Waterfront

Lake Washington Canal

In the Heart of Seattle's Chinese Community

Seattle and Mount Rainier

Fisherman Memorial at Salmon Bay Harbor

The Space Needle

Seattle Skyline

Birthplace of Seattle Monument at Alki Beach

A Sidewalk Cafe near Pioneer Square

Along the Seattle Waterfront

Seattle Skyline

University of Washington Arboretum

Replica of the Statue of Liberty at Alki Beach

Seattle Waterfront

Portage Bay from West Montlake Park

Seattle Skyline

University of Washington

Alki Point Lighthouse

Seattle Waterfront

International Fountain at Seattle Center

Pioneer Square and Smith Tower

Rose Gardens at Woodland Park

Seattle Skyline

One of Puget Sounds Ferries leaving Seattle